The Answers:
How to Increase Standardized Test Scores and Improve Discipline Management in Schools

Innovative New Strategies for School Districts, Principals, Teachers, and Parents

Ron Kelley, Ph.D.

The Answers: How to Increase Standardized Test Scores and Improve Discipline Management in Schools. 1st Edition.
© 2008 by Konfident Enterprises, LLC

Written by Dr. Ron Kelley
Edited by Dr. Ron Kelley and Elise Puente
Typed by Dr. Ron Kelley and Josefina Gonzalez

Konfident Enterprises
10004 Wurzbach #304
San Antonio, Texas 78230
(210) 954-2998
(210) 314-7137 fax
www.konfidententerprises.com

Printed in the United States of America

ISBN 978-0-6151-9692-3

3

About the Author:

Dr. Ron Kelley is a native of San Antonio, Texas. He received a Bachelor's Degree from the University of Texas at Austin, a Master's Degree from Texas State University, and a Ph.D. in Educational Administration from Texas A&M University. He is a Certified Teacher, Principal, and Superintendent. He has served as a: Technology Teacher, English Teacher, Magnet School Coordinator, Assistant Principal, Principal, Central Office Administrator, and College Professor. As a Principal, his school achieved *Gold Performance Acknowledgements*, one of Texas' highest education awards. He is the creator of the critically acclaimed *Edu-Rap* educational CD series that teaches students various academic concepts for standardized tests. The CD received national recognition by being added to the 2008 Grammy Awards ballot. The development of this innovative CD led to tremendous success for his consulting company, Konfident Enterprises. He now travels year-round providing consulting services for school districts and presenting to educators, parents, and students.

Dr. Kelley is a member of the Advisory Council for the College of Education at Texas A&M University. In the music industry, he is a member of the Recording Academy, which selects the Grammy Awards each year. He owns an independent record label that has achieved major label distribution and works with dozens of platinum recording artists. He is a member of Kappa Alpha Psi Fraternity, Inc. and is also a 33rd Degree Prince Hall Mason and Shriner. He is a Knight Templar, Royal Arch Mason, and affiliated with the Order of Eastern Star. He also holds memberships in the Improved Benevolent Protective Order of Elks of the World and the 100 Black Men of America, Inc. Dr. Kelley's future goals consist of producing more educational CD's, books, and educational materials to continue improving student achievement worldwide.

TABLE OF CONTENTS

Introduction

When I was serving as a principal and when I was teaching, I always wished that there was a comprehensive manual with all of the true strategies for student success. Well, it's in your hands now! In this book, I have compiled all of the strategies that I have seen work very effectively throughout my career in public education. This book will serve as a straight-to-the-point guide that principals, teachers, and parents can refer to for "The Answers". We will first focus on that beast that looms over all educators' heads- standardized tests! Since standardized tests appear to be the "important thing" in today's schools, we will focus on how to master them and then move on to more interesting things! We will also focus on discipline management. Since discipline management is a central issue in most schools with students in poverty, I will show you how to address discipline problems and solve them so that you can move on to what we are in schools to do- EDUCATE! This is a book that you will want to keep by your desk if you are a teacher or principal. School districts- you may want to share this information with your employees, because I am going to show you how to make some across-the-board changes that could improve your entire school district.

Overall, we will get straight to the matters at hand and skip all of the theoretical, boring stuff. I want to give you real answers for real problems that I have personally encountered and solved at some of the nation's toughest schools. You may not agree with all of my solutions or you may have already used some of them, however, I guarantee that you will walk away from this book with an arsenal of

techniques that you can use at your school TODAY.

Are you ready? All right, let's go change some

students' lives!

CHAPTER 1

Who is Dr. Ron Kelley?

Why is this book called *The Answers*? Not because I have all of the answers to every problem in today's schools. It is called *The Answers* because it presents the answers to the questions of "How do you produce immediate results?" and "How do you improve in one year or less? That has always been important to me. I have always heard people saying things about "3-year plans" and "we're going to do this by whatever date". I always have had a sense of urgency as an educator. My motto was "I need these scores now!" And even if the scores were already up, my motto was, "I need higher scores now!" So I realized that there needed to be a book that really gives parents, teachers, principals, superintendents, and everyone else a plan that's concrete and focused on things that you can really put into action.

Let me tell you about me. Any time that you read someone's book, you need to know the writer's background. Who is this that is going to take up hours of my time? So, let's talk about what qualifies me to have *The Answers*. I'm originally from San Antonio, Texas- the home of the Alamo and the World Champion San Antonio Spurs. I was raised in a middle-class home with a police officer father and a mother who was a nurse. I have one sister who is seven years older than me. My family is very close and has always been a great inspiration to me. The support that they have provided for me has been the foundation of all of my success. I have always had an interest in music. You know those kids in your school that want to be rappers? Well, I was one of those kids. However, I realized very early that the record labels were the ones making the money, not the artists. So, I started my own independent record label and built a small studio in the 6th grade. I released my first record, and I do mean an actual vinyl "record", as a junior in high school. Even though I had dreams of making it in the music industry, I still knew that education was the key to everything.

I also had a strong interest in the military. After being a successful leader in ROTC in high school, I decided to attend the US Naval Academy Preparatory School. I eventually realized that I didn't like the idea that the military would keep me so far from home, so I decided against a military career. However, that year at the Academy gave me the preparation that I have used to excel in everything that I do. I decided to attend the University of Texas at Austin. Perfect for me- great school and one hour from my hometown. I had a great time and learned a lot at UT- especially as a member of my fraternity- Kappa Alpha Psi. I graduated from UT and ended up teaching at a high school there in Austin. I was still very active in the music industry, so I managed to find a teaching assignment that was as close as possible to what I loved. It was a video production program and I would be allowed to add the music side to it. Now this was an inner-city school with some pretty tough students. There had been shootings, lots of gang activity, and many other problems at the school. The program had practically no resources, just a few pieces of outdated equipment. In two years, I developed one of the nation's top technology programs there. We had a state-of-the-art audio and video production studio and were a *Blue Ribbon* school. My program even won an award for producing a TV commercial for 7up.

I then moved on to be the coordinator of a technology magnet school in San Antonio. The school was located on the west side of San Antonio in a tough, predominantly Hispanic area. The magnet program was struggling in many ways. After I changed a few things, in one year, it became the top magnet program in the district and one of the top middle school magnet programs in the nation. By the time that I left for my next position, we had built a completely new building, exclusively for my magnet program! It looked better than the actual school! So at that that point I said, okay, I'm doing the job of a principal as the magnet coordinator, I need to be a principal! Meanwhile, I was completing my master's degree at Texas State University in San Marcos, about thirty minutes from

San Antonio. I also completed my principal certification and began the Ph.D. program at Texas A&M University in College Station, Texas. I wasn't playing around, I was preparing myself to be the best principal that I could be and trying to make it to that point as fast as possible.

I was still doing the music thing, releasing several successful CD's along the way. Meanwhile, I applied for assistant principal and received a job at the toughest school in the district- Martin Luther King Middle School. King had a history of severe discipline and academic problems and was designated by the state as a *Low-Performing* school. Working under one of my mentors, John Simpson, we cleaned up the discipline problems, pulled the school out of the *Low-Performing* rating in one year and brought in the technology component that had worked so well for me at my previous schools. We also began to really change these students' lives through powerful mentoring programs, such as the one that my Masonic lodge implemented there to work specifically with African-American males. So I figured, well, I've been an assistant principal now- I now need to be THE principal!

So after a short stint as a central office administrator, which fulfilled my superintendent internship and got me seriously thinking about being a superintendent, at the age of 31, I got my first principal assignment. Another challenging assignment, this time as the only African-American principal in the entire school district and at a school with a 99% Hispanic population on the south side of San Antonio. Within one year, we received the state's top honor of *Gold Performance Acknowledgements* in Reading, Math, and Science.

I then decided to re-locate to Houston, which had more opportunities for me in the music industry while I was completing my climb up the ladder in both education and music. I was hired for a principal position in a district that had been one of the top school districts in the state. I was assigned to bring up one of the lowest-performing schools in the district. I came in, revamped the whole program, and quickly brought the school's assessment scores up. While principal here, I came up with the idea of *Edu-Rap*, which we will discuss in a later chapter. The *Edu-Rap* project took off immediately nationwide, causing me to realize that I would be a lot happier being a national consultant since the district and I weren't seeing eye-to-eye on the type of additional changes that I wanted to see at my school. I also spoke out on some racial issues that I saw there and that put the district administration and

I in a pretty tense relationship with each other. So I resigned and plunged feet first into my goal of changing the world of education. I finished up my Ph.D. and superintendent certification and began getting requests to speak at conferences and schools nationwide. I was also appointed to a position as an adjunct professor in San Antonio and Houston, fulfilling another one of my goals- becoming a college professor. I was selected to be on the Advisory Council for the College of Education at Texas A&M, which was a great honor considering the fact that I was a recent doctoral graduate. I was also selected to receive the 33rd degree of Masonry, which was an accomplishment that I never thought that I would receive, considering the fact that many of America's greatest leaders have received that award. Meanwhile, my music career was still going strong. I owned a recording studio in Houston, was working with several platinum recording artists, had a deal on the table with one of the largest major record labels in the world, and became a member of the Recording Academy which selects the Grammy Awards each year. My *Edu-Rap* CD even ended up actually making it onto the Grammy ballot in 2008!

All of my experiences, accomplishments, challenges, successes, and failures have duly prepared me to develop the ultimate plan for today's schools. I have personally witnessed this plan change the lives of students and take schools to heights that they never imagined. Let's now explore this plan and help discover *The Answers* to the problems in today's schools.

Chapter 2

"Let's Get it Started": Understanding Students
in Poverty

First of all, to understand poverty, you must

define poverty. Not the dictionary definition, but

YOUR definition. The definition that YOU are

faced with in your school every single day. The

"poverty" that I have seen in most schools is

something that I define as, "a culture that is based

upon the environment created as a result of a family

not earning enough income to live a comfortable

lifestyle". You may define poverty in another way,

but the poverty that I have seen generally falls

under that definition. The culture of poverty

generally involves several traits that are common

among students in poverty, regardless of race. There

is usually some resistance to authority. This is due

to parents who may have had discipline problems in

school or who exhibit this type of behavior to authority figures in the presence of their children. There is also the presence of a "need for belonging". Students in poverty want to "belong". This may come about in the form of gang membership, belonging to "cliques", or identifying with a specific culture, such as hip hop. Another characteristic of poverty is a lack of exposure. These students have not been exposed to success. They have no role models around them to refer to when aiming for a goal. The final characteristic of my definition of a student in poverty is a lack of confidence. These students do not believe that they can excel because of the constant disappointments in their lives. Many of their hopes are promptly shut down due to money issues in the home, parental relationship problems, parental drug abuse, and many other factors.

RACIAL DIFFERENCES

There are definitely distinct differences between racial groups in poverty. Many educators try to overlook these issues to be "politically correct", but it is right there in their faces! Let's try not to "sugarcoat" things, let's face the facts so that we can address and fix these issues now. We all know that there are differences between racial groups in society, so why wouldn't there be differences between racial groups at a school? The faster that we can learn how to address these issues, the faster we can make some changes.

White Students

White students in poverty have certain characteristics that are very evident. Many of these students attend schools that are predominantly African-American or Hispanic. Because they are the minority in these schools, they generally play a very "low-key" role. They are mainly just trying to survive in these environments without being harassed or insulted. However, some white students assimilate very well into the African-American or Hispanic culture. It is very rare for white students to maintain their own culture in this environment. They merely assimilate or maintain an almost "invisible" role. This detachment from the school's culture usually leads to low grades and test scores. These same students would probably have much higher grades and test scores in an environment where they were the dominant culture.

The Answers- Include the students in the school's culture as much as possible. Sports and other activities can easily help this process. Once the student is known for something other than being the only "white kid", he or she will establish an identity and develop a love for the school.

African-American Students

African-American students have one of the most dominant cultures in a school environment. Many African-American students excel in sports and other activities and have some of the most outgoing personalities in the school. However, many of these same students have difficulty getting along with figures of authority. Why? Because the school fails to hold their attention! Many African-American students are very talented and creative in many ways and schools simply do not develop this talent. Many teachers and administrators don't even understand the African-American students' personalities from the beginning. This results in some teachers and administrators being "scared" of these students and puts them in a state where they are waiting to react when the students violate a rule.

The Answers- You must develop these students' talents! African-American males especially, have dominant, creative personalities. You must give these students leadership responsibilities and keep them involved in multiple activities. African-American females also have dominant, creative personalities. They must be allowed to be creative and must be challenged academically. The key to this strategy working effectively is that you must communicate with the students in an appropriate manner. These students do not respond well to yelling or derogatory language towards them. Black culture is a "give respect, get respect" culture. How do I know? Because I'm Black and I've been Black all of my life!

Hispanic Students

Hispanic students are a very important group in your school. Due to the fact that many schools nationwide are becoming predominantly Hispanic, we MUST learn how to teach Hispanic students. Many Hispanic students have a strong sense of "belonging" regarding various social groups. They usually have a close-knit group of friends that they associate with. In an environment, where they are the minority, they tend to play a reserved role similar to that discussed earlier regarding white students. In an environment where they are the majority, it is usually just a matter of communicating the school's goals to the students, and you can get these students to excel academically as a group. Many students who are from Mexico come from families that have a strong respect for education. These students will easily excel with proper support from their teachers.

The Answers- If the Hispanic students are the minority, include them! Allow them to be comfortable in their chosen groups, but also include them in all school-wide activities. When I worked at Martin Luther King Middle School, our Hispanic students had the lowest test scores compared to the other Hispanic students in the district. We eventually realized that they were not performing well because they did not feel included at the school. The school was located in a predominantly African-American area, was named after an

African-American leader, had elaborate Black History Month programs each year, it was all about African-Americans. We started including them and embracing their culture and their scores improved right away. Many times, schools let the predominantly Spanish-speaking students just exist in their own world because they don't speak English that well. Another key point is to recognize these students' potential. Many Hispanic students are capable of following the principal's lead to wherever he or she wants to take the school. If the school has low standards, these students will not excel. If the school has high standards, they will achieve the goal every time!

There are other racial groups that exist in our schools, but these three groups that we have discussed are the primary models when it comes to examining students in poverty. The techniques for addressing other groups such as: Asian, Indian, and Middle Eastern students can easily fall into any of the three categories that were discussed. Overall, we MUST recognize the differences between races, address the needs of each racial group, and then put each group in a position where they can definitely excel.

Chapter 3

"Break it Down": Breaking Down the Keys to Success on Standardized Tests

<u>The Problem</u>

We have a serious problem when it comes to standardized tests.

Problem 1: We do not adequately prepare students for standardized tests. You cannot teach one way for an entire school year and then change the format at the end of the year for some big test. We expect students to sit there and watch teachers lecture to them, go through the book, take mini-tests, and then put a "big test" in front of them that looks different, sounds different, etc.

Problem 2: We don't understand how standardized tests work. Many principals and teachers have yet to sit down and try to truly analyze the psychology behind the test. The entire way that we present standardized tests to students shows that there is a lack of understanding of how these tests really work.

Setting Goals

A school must set clear goals when it comes to standardized tests. Many times these goals are set among the staff and mentioned occasionally to the students, but they are not "goals" in the student's definition of a "goal". Schools must first understand their goals. A school should always aim for the highest possible goal academically. In Texas, the highest goal for our state test, the TAKS test, is an *Exemplary* rating. This goal requires 90% of the students in the school to pass each subject on the TAKS test. If a school truly aims for this goal of 90% and talks about it to students all day every day, it almost ensures itself a score that is out of the lower ranges. However, in order to truly accomplish this goal, the school's plan needs to be set up to actually achieve the goal. For example, a school should analyze their test results from last year and then figure out how many more students need to pass to reach 90%. Then, you identify who the "most likely passers" are and work intensely with that group. The other students will also improve by merely being in such an intense academic environment. It's as simple as that! In order to get students to buy into this goal, they need to know about the goal and what it really means. If you explain to students that an *Exemplary* rating actually makes their school superior to other schools, they can relate to that competitive spirit and they will want that type of recognition. You must mention this goal frequently and have it posted everywhere so that it becomes a part of the school's environment and culture. Overall, the staff and students must understand how to reach this goal and then hear about it every day.

School Culture and Climate

In order to achieve high test scores, the school must have a culture and climate that focuses on success every day. Teachers' attitudes should reflect the school's high standards. The school should look successful. The school should be clean and modern. How can a school be successful if it is dirty and outdated? Image and appearance is very important in setting the tone for success. Technology is an important aspect of this image. If the school has old, outdated computers that are just sitting there collecting dust, then those computers need to be moved out of the classrooms. Cluttered classrooms are also a big problem. If teachers have "junk" that they are simply not using, move it out! A clean, organized classroom's students can out-perform a messy, cluttered classroom's students every time.

In regard to the school's psychological environment regarding students, teachers should address students with respect at all times. High-performing schools ensure that they do this to keep the students' winning attitudes alive. If students are talked to in a derogatory manner, it will create an environment of failure. Students should be treated as "winners" if you want to win! However, this does not mean sacrificing an environment of strict discipline. It simply involves creating a positive environment that fosters success.

Teaching Strategies

To produce high scores on standardized tests, teachers must use certain proven methods in the classroom. The way that most teachers are teaching in today's schools is not geared toward direct success on these tests. The teaching must be a "prescription" for solving the "disease" of the test. Now I know that many say, "it shouldn't be all about the test". But let's face it, that's how our schools are being judged, so deal with it! In the classroom, teachers should base their lessons off of what appears on the test. These lessons must be taught in a manner that directly prepares students to take the test and excel on the test. Classroom lessons should be reinforced with test questions that address the skill that's being taught. What this does is prepare the student for what they will actually see on the test. For students in upper-class communities who have traveled extensively and have had parents teaching them since they were infants, this type of direct correlation may not be necessary. However, for students in poverty, you must let the students know what they need to know to pass the test, show them how to "know it", and then give them daily practice showing that they "know it".

Teachers must also find a way to keep their lessons interesting. Find out what your class is into and then base your lessons around that. This is one of the reasons that I was successful with the *Edu-Rap* CD that we will discuss in further detail later. The students are into hip hop, so if you present their lesson through a rap song, they are now into the lesson! The teacher should take the time to get to know the things that his or her class is into.

The teaching should also be very "focused". If the lesson that you are teaching has no direct relation to material on the test, find a new lesson! Each class day should be a building block to advance to success on that test. The teacher's entire year's lesson plans should be about working through the test. By the end of the year, the students should be able to breeze through any test because the teaching directly prepared them. Let the students know this also. They need to know that each day is important because it is preparing them specifically for their test. Once they realize this, this will also improve attendance because they won't want to miss any information that they know will raise their scores.

Common Mistakes

Now, let's list some of the common mistakes that schools make in regard to preparing for standardized tests.

      a. Not focusing in the classroom- the curriculum must be directly related to the test

      b. Programs- we sometimes focus on following a particular curriculum or program which has nothing to do with the test

      c. Focusing too much on discipline- discipline-plagued schools sometimes just dwell on their discipline problems and forget about the test

d. Poor data- sometimes the data that we use is too jumbled and confusing. Schools need "real data" that is clear and simple

e. Not focused "at the top"- administrators spending time on things not related to the test

To put it simple, schools must decide what they really want. If you want to excel on the test at a challenging school, you have to focus. Step out of your comfort zone and yearly routine and focus on the test. The test scores don't show your great PTA or your great band program, the scores show how well you prepared the students for the test. All of these other programs are great, but all eyes are on the school's scores. In reality, not many outsiders care about the great things going on at the school as much as they care about those test scores that are printed in the paper, announced on TV, etc. Keep the main thing the main thing!

Assessments

In order for students to pass standardized tests, they need to be familiar with the format. Many times we give students tests that look nothing like the test that they will be taking. Students do not understand this. Make sure that every assessment looks exactly like the real test. Also, these assessments need to be given on a monthly basis or even more frequently. This reduces test anxiety because students will be in a routine of taking tests. The best assessments to use are the released versions of previous tests. The environment for these assessments needs to be the exact same as the real test. If you shut everything down for the real test, shut everything down for your monthly assessments. Ensure that on the day of the real test, the students will see nothing different than that which they are already acquainted with.

When you finally have your assessment results, focus on the percentage of students passing in each class. Forget all of the other data and just focus on getting each class to at least 90% passing. This way, the data is clear and easy to understand for everyone.

CHAPTER 4

"Set it Off": Beginning The Process of Raising Standardized Test Scores

You've read about how I raised test scores at numerous schools that I worked at and the theory behind understanding students in poverty and test success. This chapter is going to tell you exactly how to improve test scores on whatever your state test is. Whether it's the state test, end of course exams, whatever the test, here's how you do it.

To the principals out there, the first key for you is to surround yourself with the best people possible. I surrounded myself with the best people and the people who could do things well that I couldn't do. I interviewed over 20 people for my assistant principal opening one year. That's how serious I was about this. I had a profile that I was looking for to create the ultimate school. I needed that exact missing piece to the puzzle. So at the top, try to form an all-star team that will lead your school to greatness.

So, here's how it all happens- The "Turn-Around Process". The first thing that you need to do is: "set your goal and set it high". Many times we say that we're aiming to improve from last year. That is not a high enough goal. Focus on whatever your state's highest rating is or simply focus on "100% passing". After you've set your goal, you have to post it everywhere. It needs to be everywhere- you need to talk about it all the time. Next, you have to look at the data- where are you now? That's the biggest thing, and it is simple. It's not about complex data tables or complicated percentages- this is how it works: Cut it down to the basics, simple questions and simple answers. Where are we now? How many non-passers do you have?

I would ask my teachers on a weekly basis, who are your non-passers? My teachers were so aware of their non-passers that these same non-passers were literally on their minds all day while they taught their classes! This alone helped many needy students receive extra attention. The teachers started teaching directly to the struggling students. When teachers teach to the non-passers, this prepares the non-passers and also enhances the preparation of everyone else. My high-scoring kids got even higher scores as my low-scoring kids improved. Focusing on the non-passers takes a big job and makes it smaller. A school of 1,000 students can be rounded down to about 200 students when you are focusing on the non-passers. You can make that "mountain" look like a mere bump in the road!

Once you've set high goals and evaluated the data, it's time to "start your engines". First, you can group the non-passers according to how many

teachers that are on the campus that do not teach

regular classes. I was lucky at one of my campuses

because I had a lot of extra teachers- "pull-out"

teachers, specialists, aides, etc. We matched up all

of the non-passers with all available staff. So that

way, every struggling student had a personal tutor

to match up with. Most principals buy supplies and

programs- I buy PEOPLE. I hired degreed substitute

teachers in each subject area. I put these teachers on

contracts that were performance-based. If you

produce results- you get to come back next year.

This was an appealing job for them because they

worked with very small groups all day and faced

zero discipline problems. I had a group of retired

teachers that worked so hard for me. They came in,

made a connection with the kids, and instead of

jumping from school to school as a sub, they would

see these same four or five kids everyday. This became the most popular sub assignment in the district because of the small class sizes. They made a connection with the kids and they made a connection with me because they really cared about their students' progress. Now, look at that, I just added an additional twenty people to my staff! "Buying" subs and "buying" other staff members was a very creative way to build the ultimate tutoring program.

Tutoring

"Whole-Day Tutoring", this is the magic formula. Everyone loves to use after-school tutoring, but that's simply not enough. I did what I call "Whole-Day Tutoring". If you are a non-passer at my school, you're going to meet with a tutor before school, you're going to meet with a tutor for one hour during school, and you're going to meet with a tutor for one hour after school. We're going to tutor you for three hours every single day that you're in this building. We're not waiting for after school, when you're tired and when the teacher is tired. The time when some teachers' focus might be just collecting one extra hour of pay…not the ideal time to produce extraordinary results, huh? Students can see that. Students know when they are not getting 110% effort from their teacher. We hit 'em with personal attention one, two, three hours everyday. Students started to think, "Dr. Kelley is kind of serious about this test thing!".

The key to the tutoring program is a concept that I created called "One-on-One 101". Basically, you get as close to "one-on-one for one hour" as you can. I know that's hard to do because of staffing issues and time, but you know the saying, "where there's a will, there's a way!" As you get closer to test time, all non-passers should be in a one hour-session each day. This one is pretty much a guarantee. If you tutor a student for one hour each day one-on-one, you can get that student to pass.

Assessments

I call it: "assessing weekly, not weakly", "W-E-E-K-L-Y", not, 'W-E-A-K-L-Y". Student progress should be assessed at least once a week. We were assessing at the campus level, not waiting for a district-level assessment. After the first three weeks of school, there should be an initial assessment. Three weeks to get things going, to get everybody in the right mode, and then assess. Some teachers were starting to test their classes right away, but the formal assessment was given three weeks in, and then every week. You may wonder how this works without burning the students out, well, a little program called "Test-Out Thursday and Fun Friday". It's all about incentives. This is how it works: every Thursday, you should give a mini-test, not too long, a couple of key questions for each subject. If a student passes this test, he /she can participate in "Fun Friday". "Fun Friday" can be a dance, pizza party, field day, basketball tournament, whatever your students like. If a student does not pass the test, they cannot participate in "Fun Friday". They go to a tutoring session while the other students are at "Fun Friday". This session should be close enough to the "Fun Friday" location so that the students can hear the other students having fun. This works! Try this- and you'll eventually have every student in "Fun Friday". They will do whatever they can to not miss out on the fun. Regarding the students that don't get to participate, you're not punishing them for not passing, you're just giving them extra tutoring time. You probably won't have to do that twice! Once they miss out one time and hear all that fun going on in the gym or wherever, they will do whatever they need to do to get over there next week!

One important fact about assessments that we mentioned earlier is that you must use released versions of the actual state test. Any test that does not look like the real test is a waste of time. Students in poverty perform best when they know what the real test looks like. By testing students with a released version of the test on a weekly basis, you can eliminate most anxiety on the actual test day. Familiarity with the format is the key. If your assessment days are just like the real test- the students are calm, the teachers are calm, everyone will be calm on test day.

An effective use of elective classes and non-tested subject areas is also important. If elective courses also participate in preparing the school for testing, it will only enhance the school's overall performance. While I was a middle school administrator, the school's coach had a system that was the best example of this. He requested a classroom next to the gym. When his class started, the students would report to the classroom where he would give them a short test that contained a few questions from each subject area. The students' main objective in gym class every day was to get a chance to play basketball. To get to the gym to play basketball, they had to pass these short tests. Every student started passing these tests! Special education students, bilingual students, everyone! The desire to go play basketball was stronger than any of the deficiencies that they supposedly had.

This was phenomenal. This basically means that if the incentive is strong enough, any student can achieve any academic goal. Students who couldn't read that well previously were reading pretty well all of a sudden to go to the gym and play basketball! Unfortunately, the coach passed away that school year. He was a great educator and mentor for the students. The staff at King Middle School will never forget Coach Wayland Gay.

Mentoring

Every student on a school campus needs a mentor. I matched up every student with an adult on my campus. Thirty minutes per week is all that you need for an effective mentoring program. These mentoring sessions were not your typical "how's your home life?" sessions. My groups focused on

test-taking skills. I know this sounds different- but it's the perfect time to address a skill that will directly affect scores. A skill that we usually wait until the last minute to discuss. Test-taking skills need to be discussed all year long! Mentors should talk with students about ways to relax, breathing properly to relax, eating breakfast before testing, everything regarding how to take tests.

Competition

Competition is the key to making assessments count. Friendly competition can be easily created with class ranking charts. This is a weekly chart that ranks each class and its performance on assessments. At first, scores will be low and teachers don't like this. The charts should be given to all teachers so that they can see where each class ranks. Sometimes, the tears come out from the teachers at this point, you know that "we hate the principal/we hate this school" feeling that some teachers get. You know that, "this guy is all about the test" and that "we're just teaching the test" feeling, all because the scores were low and everyone saw them. This was always interesting because I knew how the feelings switched once we were successful. How do you think the scores were on the second list? 100% of the students passed in this class, 98% in this class, 95% in this class, etc. The method is uncomfortable at first, but it gets the results and eases in a love for winning among the teachers. Teachers would start coming by my office, not as a group, but mainly one-on-one. They were like, "Dr. Kelley...I see what you're doing here and I like it. Kids are progressing." I would just say, "keep plugging away and you will see more and more success every day". It takes just a short while to develop this mentality. It's very simple- you must put the students' success first. Forget about our feelings and comfort zones as adults, put the students first. We work for them. Who cares about your name being associated with low scores and the fact that everyone saw the scores? I'm personally embarrassed as the principal if the teachers don't score high, it makes me look bad too. If you're embarrassed for being number eight on a list of 8 classes, as a principal, I'm embarrassed if my school is the 8th ranked school out of 8 schools in the district. Everyone catches the heat when it comes to not performing well on standardized tests. So, to increase performance- create competition. It's not all fun and it's not all painful. Everyone wins at the end of the process.

Being that my campus was so competitive, you would think that teachers would want to transfer to another school. How many transfers do you think that I had at the end of the year? Zero. I definitely thought that I would lose a few due to the competitive nature of the environment that we created. I planned to bring in a crew of new superstar teachers to create the ultimate campus. Zero transfers- why? That was because we were the number one school in the district now. People want to be a part of a winning team.

Teaming is also a key competition-based strategy to raise scores. This is popular in high schools, but it also works very well in middle schools and even elementary schools. If a school has at least two assistant principals, it can work really well. If the assistant principals want to be principals and are truly ready to move up, that makes it even better. Basically, the school should be divided into teams based on how many assistant principals there are. Then these teams compete on all levels, with an assistant principal in charge of each team. They literally have their own school with their team. Because my assistant principals really wanted to be principals, they took this opportunity and ran with it. The competition between the teams made students and teachers perform better as a whole.

Incentives

Incentives for the students are also very important. You have to "pay" students to perform. Not with money, but with fun activities and prizes. Every goal should be linked to some kind of way to reward students for accomplishing the goal. Ideally, students should want to excel just because it is best for their future, but do you want to count on that? I don't think so. Be realistic and give them something fun to work towards. I called mine "The Ultimate School Day". It was a day where we would take a whole day to let the students play video games, have a dance, all the stuff that they like. You have to talk about this day all year long. That's all we talked about, "The Ultimate School Day". Everyone who passes the test gets to participate. Now, everyone would be allowed to participate anyway because it would be too cruel to exclude students based on test scores. But the fact that students thought that they needed to pass to ensure attending, this alone made many struggling students work much harder. This works because it is a goal that students can actually see themselves achieving. Make them strive for a goal that they can see, touch, and feel.

You also have to "pay" teachers to produce results. We all know that teachers do their job every day with the best interests of the students in mind, but a few incentives here and there for a little extra motivation don't hurt a bit! Simple things like, the teachers with 90% passing or better get a half-day off to go shopping. A principal can get creative and have the other winning teachers cover each other's classes so that other teachers can take off. There are many ways to do it. Another idea could be that the grade level that performs the best can win a 2-hour lunch at a restaurant. Anything nice like that will work! Put some of these ideas in motion at your school and watch the results magically appear right in front of you!

Chapter 5

"Crunch Time": Preparing for "The Big Day"

Once a school is set up with all of the things from Chapter 3, now it's time to prepare for the time leading up to test day. Schools must "prepare with flair!" One week before any district assessment or standardized test, the school should focus on whatever subject is going to be tested. This doesn't mean neglecting the other subjects, just focusing on the subject that matters right now. Take sports for example, if the Dallas Cowboys play the New England Patriots next week, who do they prepare for? The New England Patriots! Why would they prepare for every team in the NFL when they could focus on the task at hand and increase their chances of winning this particular game? Students living in poverty perform best when they focus on the task at hand, not future tasks that do not matter right now.

If they're going to take a reading test next week, they don't want to hear about science. Now you can throw in some science through reading exercises, but they want to get focused- so you should get focused. They want to know, "what do I have to do and what am I getting for doing it?" This focus should increase heavily the day before the test. This should be an intensive day where the tested subject is the focus of everything. The Saturday before the test is also a good time to get students focused. Saturdays are usually a bad time to do any meaningful tutoring (don't tell some schools that, they REALLY believe in Saturday tutoring!), but the Saturday before the test is a great tool that can be used to merely raise awareness of the big test coming up the following week.

The day before the test should include a large pep rally-type motivational event. Pep rallies are what we use to motivate athletes. As we know, sports have a high value to many students in poverty. If a test can be compared to the importance of a big game, you can send a message to everyone that it is time to get serious about this test. This can't be the typical "before the test" small rally that most schools do. This should be more like a high school football pep rally when the team is about to play in the state championship! A middle school or elementary school can bring in the high school football players, cheerleaders, etc. Make that connection between sports and academics. Making that connection makes students competitive and will make them take the test more seriously. In basketball, if you hit 30 points in the game, you're the star. Well, stress to the students that you have to pass all areas of the test to be the star at this school. The fun part for me now is that we do motivational rallies at schools all over the nation to motivate students to excel on their tests. Along with my hip hop DJ- Def Jam Blaster, our rallies have become some of the most popular events at schools nationwide. The rallies prepare the students with various test taking tips and techniques and leave them extremely motivated, all while using what they love- hip hop. The rallies usually book up very fast each year and many schools that have used them have seen some incredible gains on their test scores.

Test Day

The actual day of the test should be a relaxed time. The first step in this process is to have a motivational breakfast. Everyone from the principal on down should sit down and eat with the students that morning. This is also a good way to make sure that all students eat breakfast. In order to leave the cafeteria, you have to show your tray. The students walk up to the trash receptacle, the principal is standing there, and they show their tray. "Did you eat everything?", "Hey, go back and eat that piece of sausage right there". Sounds extreme, but as we all know, breakfast is a student's brain fuel. These are just a few tips for the preparation phase. If you prepare wisely, you WILL see results. Trust me!

Chapter 6

"Conquering the Discipline Monster": No Discipline- No High Test Scores

Now, on to the thing that we are all looking for answers for. My next book is entirely focused on this. Discipline. We have been talking about academics, but the way to really get the academics straight is to get the discipline straight. First things first, have a zero tolerance policy for negative behaviors- and make it known. No exceptions, no excuses, no low expectations, just make it happen. You don't have time to play around with discipline. There is no time for discipline problems if you want high test scores. Consistent consequences is the key. Make these known through a highly visible discipline plan. If you fight- here's what happens, if you're tardy- this is what happens, etc. Plain and simple- make the consequences firm and follow them to the letter. If your school has a problem with fighting- eliminate it. Here's an example of how you eliminate a discipline problem: for fights, I call it my "Three and Three" Plan. If you fight, or even look like you're going to fight, you get suspended for 3 days. When you come back, you have 3 days of in-school suspension AND you get issued a citation from the school police officer for disorderly conduct. Do this right and fights will disappear. Students do not want to be out of school and away from their friends for six days- no matter what! Parents do not want to pay a ticket because their kid was at school acting a fool! Zero tolerance works. The elementary level is not an exception. The punishments may be slightly different, but the environment should still be firm and very consistent.

A good in-school suspension (ISS) program is very important. As a principal, I always ensured that I had an efficient ISS program going. Forget about that "just sit by the principal's office". Get a room in a good location, face the desks toward the walls, get your program going right! You must have a good, strong teacher in there- a teacher that the kids really respect. An indication that your ISS is pretty good is when students simply do not want to go. When you say, "you're going to ISS", you should hear, "No! I don't want to go! Suspend me!" Good quality tutoring can also happen in ISS. The teacher gets to work one-on-one with each student while all of the other students are sitting there working quietly until it's their turn to be tutored.

Here's another key discipline component. To maintain a high level of discipline, the students need time to relax. Lunch is the key to this. Have a relaxed cafeteria, have firm classrooms. I call it my "RC/FC Method"-relaxed cafeteria/firm classrooms. My cafeteria was a fun place for the students. I know that many administrators like to be really strict in the cafeteria, not me. All you had to do in the cafeteria was not throw food and stay in your seat. I let the students enjoy lunch, talk, laugh, anything within reason. You know why? Because when they stepped out of the cafeteria, they had released all of their energy and were ready to get serious for class. How can we ask students to be 100 % focused all of the time? Adults can't even do that. During lunch, teachers go into the lounge, unwind, talk about the principal, talk about each other, you know how teachers do. Principals get their lunch, close the door, get on the phone, browse the internet, basically unwind for a minute. We do whatever we need to do to relax for a few minutes so that we can get through the rest of the day. We take a few minutes off during the day- we chill. How can you expect a student to sit there while someone's yelling on a microphone and walking around watching their every move? Then, they have to go back to class and focus some more. Not a good plan. It is OK for students to be loud while they eat. As long as they stay in their seats, most problems are avoided. Some students living in poverty may sometimes seem a little "extra loud" to you. First, understand their situation. If you lived in a 2-bedroom apartment with 15 people, you might talk loud too! In the African-American culture, when we eat, we like to talk. That's our time to communicate, and some of us decide to talk very loud during this time! In our culture, there's a lot of value in strength of voice. If you talk quietly and kind of mumble, that's a sign of weakness. A strong voice focuses all attention on you. In a poverty-stricken home, good conversation is your entertainment. You should consider all of these sociological factors before you label a student as "disrespectful" or "disruptive". Students are willing to be quiet in class knowing that they get their lunch time to sit there and talk and have fun. So remember that RC/FC method!

Attendance

Attendance is a key component of discipline management. It is crucial to achieving high test scores. You must work really hard on your attendance rate. Here's how you get them there- plain and simple. Give away something that they like. Every month, I gave away an Xbox. We held a drawing that had every student's name that had perfect attendance, the students would go crazy over this! One student would win and the rest would still be excited and eager to win next month. Everyone was coming to school every day to win that Xbox! The crazy thing is that they already had one at home! They just wanted to win one in front of everyone at school. Surprise events also work. I call it "if you miss it, you missed it." Have different fun events that just pop up with no warning. If you weren't at school that day, you just totally missed out. They didn't know what to expect and it may be as simple as giving away cool pencils that day. Something small, but everyone wanted to be there for those surprise events. If you can get all of your students to come to school every day- behavior will improve and scores will definitely improve- you knew that!

Chapter 7

"Making That Connection": The Hip Hop Generation

Now it's time for the "icing on the cake".

That's what I call this part. The connection. All of

this that I've said in this book is meaningless if you

don't know how to connect with students. The

quickest, easiest way to connect with students is

through their culture. There is one dominant culture

among today's students- hip hop. As you already

know, hip hop doesn't just involve the African-

American students. It is the culture of almost all of

today's students. Hip hop culture consists of four

elements: rapping, breakdancing, DJ'ing, and

graffiti art. Hip hop was developed in the late

1970's in the Bronx, New York. It has since grown

from a small, New York fad to a multi-billion dollar

international phenomenon. As you know, hip hop is

in movies, commercials, churches, everywhere! Being that I have a music background and have worked in the hip hop industry, I knew that using hip hop culture in a positive way in schools would be the "magic touch" to getting test scores higher. I came up with this concept called "Edu-Rap". It consists of a CD with a rap song for every subject that students are tested on. Each song teaches the students concepts that they need to pass that subject on their state tests. I knew that it was a hit when I gave a sample copy to my music teacher one day. I walked by her classroom and the students came running out of the classroom. They were like, "is that you? That is so cool!" Here's a sample of the lyrics to one of the songs on the CD. This particular song is designed to help students pass the reading exam. Check it out:

"I Can Read More Than You"

It's time to talk about the most important skill,
This is the skill, that pays the bills,
The one you need, every minute of the day,
Without this skill, hey yo, there is no way,
To do anything, anything at all,
You need it winter, summer, autumn, spring, and
fall,
I'm talking about reading, the #1 thing,
You have to read to rap, and read to sing,
You have to read the plays in football or hoops,
You have to read if you're a part of the military
troops,
So get in the habit, read everyday,
The more you read, the more you pay,
Your mind, it's like money in the bank,
Every time you read, you fill up your think tank,
Read aloud, read outside,
Read to Mom, read with pride,
Get your read on, the E. Ron way,
Look at your friends, and I want you to say,

Chorus- Yo, I can read more than you,
I can read more than you,
I can read more than you, you, you, and you

Read anything you want, live in the library,
Everywhere you go, a book you should carry,
Now you're gonna have to take reading tests,
So here's some tips, so you can do your best,
The main idea will get you an A,
It's what every paragraph is trying to say,
Compare and contrast, the name of the game,

Check what is different and what is the same,
Who are the characters? What is the title?
What's the story about? this is vital,
That means important, know your vocabulary,
Going a day without reading, now that's scary,
January, February, March, April, May,
Every single month, we read, look at your friends
and say
(repeat chorus)

This song became a hit all over the nation and has helped many students improve their reading scores just like that, using a rap! In Texas, the 5th grade science exam is seen as one of the toughest state tests. Schools are looking for any way to improve their science scores. This is what I came up with that has helped many schools improve their science scores. Check out how the science song teaches the student many of the concepts that he/she needs for the test:

"The Science Chant"

It's time for some science yall,
If you listen close, you'll be able to do it all,
In the lab, the first rule is safety,
This is important, so you can make the,
Lab safe for you, lab safe for me,
Can't run in the lab, cause we're accident free,
Now you know safety, the #1 rule,
Now let's get to know a few lab tools,
A thermometer does what, finds temperature,
If you learn the lab, one day, you might find the
cure,
For diseases, discover new things for helping,
When a solid turns to liquid, that's melting,
Carnivore, meat eater, herbivore, plant eater,
Gotta know about milliliters and millimeters,
Gotta know the planets, so let's get with them,
First we're gonna talk about the inner solar system,
Mercury, Venus, Earth, and Mars,
These are closest to the Sun, we don't wanna be far,
The Sun provides the heat and light we need,
Now here's the outer solar system, yes indeed,
Jupiter, Saturn, Uranus, Neptune and Pluto,
Now let's go back and see what all you know,
If you know the planets, say em after me,
Mercury, Venus, Earth, Mars,
Jupiter, Saturn, Uranus, that's far,
Neptune and Pluto complete the deal,
Now you know the planets, tell me how you feel,

Smart, tell your friends, don't hate,
When water disappears, it evaporates,
Sunlight and water go into a plant,
And oxygen comes back out of the plant,
Sound is caused by vibrations,

Science is done in all nations,
Water boils at 212° Fahrenheit,
Water freezes at 32° Fahrenheit,
When water boils, a liquid becomes a gas,
Gravity makes rain drop down fast,
Now you know science, so don't ever say I can't,
Now it's time to say the Science Chant,

Chorus- Science is something I gotta have,
Teacher, Teacher, Teacher, let's go to the lab,
Science is you,
Science is me,
S-C-I-E-N-C-E,
Is so cool,
Is so tight,
Give me a science test, I'll get 'em all right!

This song takes many challenging concepts from science and puts them in a fun format for students to learn. The *Edu-Rap* CD has motivated many students to learn because it puts what they need to know in the way that they want to learn it. Hip hop is the key to connecting with today's students. Get on the hip hop band wagon or get left behind!

Conclusion

So that's all folks. If you even do just a few of the things that we talked about, you will see major results from your students. OK, a quick review: Remember, for all standardized tests- aim high and prepare for the test every day. For discipline management- be firm, consistent, and make sure that you connect with the students and their culture. Creating a great school or great classroom is easy if you have a "plan". I visit schools all of the time that have a "plan" and are seeing results from it. You might even see me on your campus one day. I do high-energy staff development sessions for principals and teachers and we also do the motivational rallies for students year-round all over the nation. Get your students into the *Edu-Rap* CD and workbook too. They work! Now stop reading and go out and change some lives, you now have

THE ANSWERS!

Dr. Ron Kelley

drronkelley@konfidententerprises.com

www.konfidententerprises.com

NOTES

<u>NOTES</u>

<u>NOTES</u>

NOTES

<u>NOTES</u>